Monkey Business

Written by Barbara Winter
Illustrations by Esme Nichola Shilletto

DOMINIE PRESS
Pearson Learning Group

Editor: Bob Rowland
Author: Barbara Winter
Illustrator: Esme Nichola Shilletto

Copyright © 2005 by Rubicon Publishing, Inc. This edition of *Monkey Business* is published by Pearson Education, Inc., publishing as Dominie Press, an imprint of Pearson Learning Group, 299 Jefferson Road, Parsippany, NJ 07054, by arrangement with Rubicon Publishing, Inc. All rights reserved. No part of this book may be reproduced or transmitted in any form or by any means, electronic or mechanical, including photocopying, recording, or by any information storage and retrieval system, without permission in writing from the publisher. For information regarding permission(s), write to Rights and Permissions Department.

ISBN 0-7685-0745-6
Printed in Singapore
1 2 3 4 5 6 7 8 9 10 09 08 07 06 05

1-800-321-3106
www.pearsonlearning.com

Table of Contents

Chapter One
Tornado! 5

Chapter Two
Who Did It? 9

Chapter Three
Going Bananas 15

Chapter Four
Just an Angel 21

Chapter Five
Monkey Business 25

Chapter Six
Diaper Day 32

Chapter Seven
Angel Takes Off 37

Chapter Eight
Mystery Solved! 41

Chapter Nine
Captured! 48

Chapter Ten
Rescue Mission 54

Talapoin Monkey Fact Sheet 63

Using a Dictionary 64

Chapter One

Tornado!

What a Friday morning! I had a math quiz in the morning, and after recess I presented my oral book report. Both were disasters. I wasn't happy, but I *was* very hungry, when my younger brother, Max, and I arrived home for lunch.

The smell of grilled cheese greeted us. Wonderful! Grilled cheese sandwiches are my favorite lunch, after hot dogs. Mom put the sizzling sandwiches beside the carrot and celery sticks on our plates as we sat down at the kitchen table. I took a gulp of milk. "Thanks, Mom. I really needed this," I said. "I've had the worst day!"

"I thought you might need cheering up, Jake," Mom said. "How was the math test?"

"Brutal." I took a bite of my grilled cheese before adding,

"And when I gave my book report, I dropped the folder, and everything fell out. All the pages were messed up."

"I told you to staple it, *always*," Max said, as the melting cheese dribbled out of his mouth and down his chin. I glared at him.

"Well, everyone laughed, and I used up half my time picking things up, so it wasn't so bad. Mrs. Simka said my content was okay, but as usual, my delivery needed work."

"I always staple," Max piped up again with an annoying smile. "Don't I, Mom?"

I was about to give him a kick, when I remembered something. "My library book! Mrs. Lee told me this morning that I *have* to take it back today. Have you seen it, Mom?"

"If you mean the rocket book, then I last saw it in your room on the desk."

I stuffed the last bit of gooey cheese into my mouth, grabbed a handful of carrot sticks, and ran upstairs. The door to my room was shut. I pushed it open and stared in

disbelief. I was too stunned to move or open my mouth to say anything. My room looked like it had been hit by a tornado!

My posters were lying on the floor; some of them were crushed, and others were ripped into long strips. One blind had fallen off the window, and the other blind was hanging from one side. Half my books were sideways on the shelves, and the rest were scattered across the floor. My markers were tossed all over the desk and the bed. I gulped. Finally, I found my voice and yelled, "Mom! Max! Come up here now, please!"

Max charged up the stairs, chewing a carrot.

"What's the matter?" he mumbled. "Mom's busy." He stopped short at the door. His mouth dropped open. For once, he was speechless.

"Were you in my room?" I snarled.

He looked at me with raised eyebrows. "C'mon! I was at school all morning!"

I knew that, but I couldn't imagine what had caused such a disaster.

Max scratched his head. "What the heck happened here? Wait until Mom sees this!"

Suddenly, a thought struck him. "Yikes! I hope my room's okay," he yelled as he ran over to his room to check. I heard his loud whistle of relief, "Whew!"

Chapter Two

Who Did It?

When Max returned to my room, he was wearing his detective hat and carrying a notebook, a pencil, and a large magnifying glass. He was still munching on the carrot.

"What are you up to?" I asked.

"This is a real mystery," Max replied. "To solve it, we must examine all the clues."

"You look stupid," I said as I started to pick up the torn posters. Some of them could be fixed, but others were completely ruined.

"Don't touch anything," Max said. "You have to leave everything the way it is at the scene of a crime. You should really take some photos. Then we should collect evidence."

Everyone knows that Max is a smart kid, but sometimes he can be a real pain.

"Max! Just help me clean up this mess!" I told him. "I can't leave my room like this, and I don't want photos of it like this, either. Come on, give me a hand."

I picked up some of the pencils and markers that had been thrown all over my bed and across the floor.

"Hey! This is weird!" I said.

"What's weird?" echoed Max.

"Look! All my pencils and markers have been chewed on. See the teeth marks?"

Max dropped all his stuff on my bed. He took one of the pencils and examined it. Then he held the pencil up to my mouth and said, "Smile."

"What's the matter with you?" I snapped, pushing his hand away. "Stop acting silly!"

"I'm not!" Max shouted. "I'm comparing the marks on this pencil with your teeth. Maybe you're the one who did this."

"Get that pencil out of my face!" I yelled. "And stop being idiotic! I sometimes chew the ends of my pencils,

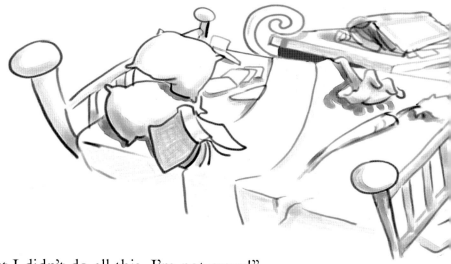

but I didn't do all this. I'm not crazy!"

Suddenly, Max noticed the amazing dictionary sitting on my desk. He hit his head with his hand. "Of course! The dictionary! Do you think a beaver could have gotten loose from your amazing dictionary? Beavers like to chew things."

"Oh no!" I breathed. "Not the amazing dictionary at work again!"

Uncle Cyrus had given me the dictionary for my tenth birthday. When I accidentally tapped on a picture of a penguin in it, a penguin appeared in my closet. Max, my older sister, Amanda, and I had had a few crazy days

hiding the penguin from our parents.

I folded my arms and glared at Max.

"I thought I told you not to touch my dictionary, ever!" I was really mad now.

"I didn't touch it!" Max was equally mad. "You know I never come into your room!"

"Then who did?" I demanded.

Max shook his head. "It sure wasn't me! Do you have mice camping in your room?"

"Don't be a fool!" I said.

Max sat down on my bed. Suddenly, he shouted, "Hey! Where's my carrot?"

"Your carrot?" I said. "Where was it?"

"Right here on the bed. With my notebook and pencil."

We both stared at the bed. While we had been looking at the pencils on my desk, the carrot had disappeared. We definitely had a mystery visitor in our midst.

Just then, Mom called out, "Boys! You'd better leave now or you'll be late!"

"What now?" Max asked.

"We'll just have to go," I said. "I'll close the door again so whatever it is can't get out and make a mess in the rest of the house."

Chapter Three

Going Bananas

All afternoon at school, my mind was on the animal running wild in my room and doing more damage. It could only have come from Uncle Cyrus's amazing dictionary. But I hadn't called it up, and neither had Max. That left Amanda, my sister. *Wait until I see her!* I thought.

Amanda was already home when we returned after school. She was having a snack with her friend Molly, so I couldn't ask her if she'd done anything with the amazing dictionary.

"I hope you haven't eaten all the cookies," I said, taking the lid off the cookie jar.

"We left you a few crumbs," Amanda said, grinning widely. Molly giggled.

I tipped the jar over and some crumbs trickled out onto my hand. I licked them up.

"You're gross!" Amanda said in disgust.

I grabbed a banana from the fruit basket and went up to my room. Max followed me, chomping on his own banana. He came through the door and carefully closed it behind him.

The room was even messier than before. The mystery animal had completely removed the second blind from the window and thrown the rest of my books out of the bookcase.

"Where's my stuff?" Max asked. He put his banana on my desk and searched around the bed. The magnifying glass was on the floor, smudged with little paw prints. The first few pages of the notebook were missing. Max picked up his things and reached for his banana.

"Not again," he yelled.

"What's wrong now?" I asked.

"Bananas!" Max shouted. "I'm the one going bananas!

The creature took my banana!" He was jumping up and down in frustration. He flopped down on my bed and picked up his notebook.

"I'm going to list all the information we have so far about this animal," he said. "Then we'll be able to figure out what it is."

Max started his list.

1. Likes carrots
2. Likes bananas
3. Climbs
4. Moves fast
5. Destroys things
6. Quiet
7. Small (we think)

Max stopped and chewed on his pencil.

"Well, what's your deduction, Sherlock?" I asked him. I folded my arms and raised my eyebrows.

"Ee-aa-sy," Max drawled. "It's a monkey."

I always knew Max was a bright kid.

"That's exactly what I was thinking!" I said excitedly. "Let's go find it!"

I waved my banana in the air, pretending it was a sword. Suddenly, a brown blur of a ball shot out from behind my desk and grabbed the whole banana right out of my hand.

"Hey! Did you see that?" I barely whispered.

"Faster than a speeding bullet!" Max said. "Wow! You've got Super Monkey in your room!"

I whispered to Max to stay still. I crept forward to look around the edge of the desk. In the far corner against the wall was a tiny greenish-brown monkey with white around its face. It was crouched on the floor, eating my banana. Max's banana peel lay beside it.

We were right! The amazing dictionary had somehow sent a monkey into my room! It was a strange-looking creature, not at all like the monkeys I had seen in the zoo. Slowly, I reached out my hand to touch it. The monkey jumped onto the desk and then bounced over to the shelf above my bed.

"She's just afraid of us," Max said. "What are we going to do with her?"

"We'll have to send her back, of course." I said. "Look how much trouble she's caused already."

Chapter Four

Just an Angel

Just then, I heard Amanda coming upstairs. I opened the door. "Get in here," I hissed.

"What's wrong?" she asked as she entered. I shut the door quickly behind her and watched as her eyes widened with alarm.

"Wait until Mom sees this!" she gasped. "What have you guys been up to in here?"

"Okay, Amanda. Stop pretending," I said. "We know what you did. Now send it back."

"What are you talking about? You can't think I did this to your room?"

"Maybe not you. But the monkey you called up from the amazing dictionary sure did," Max said.

"What monkey?" Amanda asked. "Are you sick? I really

don't know what you two are yapping about."

She turned to leave.

"Oh come on, Amanda. It's not funny anymore," I shouted. "I know you called up a monkey from the amazing dictionary just to bug me."

"For your information, Jake, I left for school with Molly before you were even out of bed. So how did I whip up a monkey without being anywhere near your precious dictionary?"

"That's right," Max said. "Molly came for her early this morning. And you were still in your room."

"I don't know how it happened, then," I said. "But I've sure got a monkey."

"Where is it?" Amanda asked.

I pointed to the shelf. The monkey had squeezed itself behind my sports trophies with its head peering around the biggest one.

"Oh, what a little sweetie," Amanda purred. She put out her arm and the monkey jumped from the shelf onto her shoulder. It snuggled into her hair and nibbled an ear.

"She's so cute!"

"If she's so cute, you can keep her in your room, Amanda," I said quickly.

"Sure. She wouldn't mess it up, would you, little diddums?" Amanda cooed.

Diddums! That monkey was a large-scale disaster, more like Godzilla on the loose.

"We can't keep it," I told Amanda. "We'll have to identify it and send it back at once."

"Can't I have her overnight?" Amanda whined. "I'll make sure she doesn't get into any trouble."

"Better take my handcuffs," I said. "You can see what she's done already."

"She'll be an angel with me," Amanda sighed. "Won't you, Angel? That's what I'm going to call you."

The monkey looked at me with its bright eyes, the way

Max does when he's trying to get me into trouble with Mom or Dad.

"I think you're making a big mistake, but you're welcome to keep her," I said with relief.

Just then, Dad shouted from the kitchen, "Kids! Dinner's ready! Wash your hands and come on down, right now!"

We took Angel over to Amanda's room and left her in the laundry basket. Amanda put some books on top of the basket to make sure she wouldn't get out. Then we all trooped downstairs for dinner.

Chapter Five

Monkey Business

At the table, Amanda announced that she wasn't eating any more meat.

"What next!" Dad said. "Remember when you boys went through that fish phase?"

We sure did. That was when I first received the amazing dictionary and Penny the penguin came into our lives. We needed all kinds of seafood to feed Penny.

"I remember," I said. "But we got over it quickly, Dad."

"But Amanda, why have you decided not to eat meat?" Mom asked.

Amanda replied slowly, "Well, I think it's wrong to eat living things."

"Carrots are living until you kill them in boiling water," Dad joked.

"That's different," Max broke in. "Carrots don't have brains."

"I've known carrots with more brains than some of the people I work with," Dad muttered. "You could replace my sales division with turnips and never notice the difference." It was obvious he'd had a bad day at the office.

"You really shouldn't give up meat, Amanda," Mom said. "When you are young and growing, you need protein."

"That's the main thing in meat," Max added. "Our teacher, Mr. Sandhu, told us about it."

"You can eat other food that's high in protein," Amanda said. "Like beans."

"I'm not sitting next to you at the table if you're going to eat lots of beans," I said.

Mom still looked worried. "We should find out more about vegetarian diets," she said. "Let's get some books from the library this weekend."

"Well, just for now," Amanda said, "I'm going to eat lots of vegetables and fruit."

"That's great," I said. "Maybe you'll stop hogging all the cookies after school."

Amanda rolled her eyes at me. She pushed her pork chop to the side of her plate and took more carrots and peas.

"If you're not going to eat that chop, I'll have it," I said. "I'm really starving because someone ate all the cookies after school."

I took a big mouthful of meat. "Oh, this is soooo gooood," I said, smacking my lips.

Amanda looked enviously at my plate. I knew she loved pork chops with applesauce.

After dinner, Max helped me clean up my room. Every now and then, we heard a thump from Amanda's room and her agitated voice. Max and I grinned. Angel was behaving badly.

"Amanda will change Angel's name to Monster very soon," I said. "And I'll bet she'll want to send her back by morning."

"That could be a problem," Max said.

"Problem? What problem?" I asked.

"Well, we still don't know how Angel got here. And we don't even know what sort of monkey she is. So, how can we find the page where her picture is?"

He was right, as usual. I opened the amazing dictionary and looked up the word *monkey*.

"What does it say?" Max asked.

I read the definition: "A primate, except lemurs, apes, and humans."

"Is there a drawing beside the words?"

"No drawing. But the next words are about monkey business, which means foolish tricks and mischief. That sure describes Angel."

An extra loud thump and a squeal came from Amanda's room. Max flashed a wicked grin.

"C'mon, Jake! Let's go and check out the monkey business next door."

We cautiously opened Amanda's bedroom door. Angel was swinging on the drapes, dropping pieces of plum onto the windowsill. Amanda's stuffed animals were scattered on the floor. Her shoes and books had been tossed around the room. Amanda was stuffing socks and underwear into a drawer.

"Shut the door!" she snapped. "Don't let her out."

Max whistled. "Having fun?" he asked.

"She's a bit excited," Amanda said. "She'll settle down soon and go to sleep."

"You hope," I said. "Better take your posters down before Angel does it for you."

Amanda yelled just as Angel leaped across her favorite Rascal Flatts poster.

Max was looking closely at something on the windowsill. "Gross!" he snorted.

"What's wrong?" I asked

Max made a face. "Amanda, did you feed Angel a lot of food?"

"Two plums, a banana, and a carrot so far," she said. "Why do you want to know?"

"I wouldn't give her any more if I were you," Max said in his know-it-all voice.

"Why not?" Amanda asked him.

"Because all the food has to go somewhere, and she's gone right here already." He pointed to the windowsill.

"Oh no!" Amanda shrieked. "Disgusting! She's pooped down my window! Yuck! Yuck! Yuck! You'll have to help me clean it up."

"No way," Max and I said together.

"You wanted her here tonight, remember? Well, she's all yours," I said. On that note, I left. And Max was right on my heels.

Chapter Six

Diaper Day

Amanda must have had a bad night. I woke up at six o'clock when I heard a knock against my wall. That was the signal that Amanda wanted help. I got out of bed, quietly opened my door, and slipped into my sister's room.

It was a wreck. You'd think that space aliens had landed and attacked her room.

"How did she make such a mess?" I whispered.

Amanda sighed tiredly. "She slept for about fifteen minutes all night. She managed to get out of the laundry basket. You were right. We have to get rid of this beast. Fast!"

I wanted to say, "I told you so," but I felt sorry for Amanda. She looked desperate. The monkey had pooped in several places, and Amanda was cleaning the walls and the floor.

"She needs a diaper," I said.

"How could we get one to fit her?" Amanda asked. "Look at her. She's tiny."

Angel jumped up onto Amanda's shoulder, looking angelic. She made a gentle chattering sound. Suddenly, Amanda said, "I've got it! We can make some diapers with grocery bags. We can cut a piece of plastic for the outside and use masking tape to hold it together. Then we can pad the inside with tissues."

I went down to the kitchen to get the masking tape and some white plastic grocery bags. Amanda and I made a couple of diapers before we got one that held together.

"Now for the big problem," I said. "How are we going to put it on Angel?"

Angel had been very interested in our work. Twice she stole the roll of masking tape, and we had to chase her to get it back. The second time she threw it at me and it hit my head.

Amanda waved the last banana and coaxed Angel down

from the windowsill. While she was eating, Amanda held her down and I fitted the diaper around her. It looked funny, but when she jumped onto the desk, the diaper stayed on.

Amanda threw an old shirt into the laundry basket, and Angel snuggled into it. We taped the lid down with masking tape and pushed the laundry basket into the closet. Then we piled books on top of the basket. Now

Angel wouldn't be able to get out.

"She's tired," Amanda said. "No wonder, after last night. I'd like to go back to bed, too, but I have to tidy up before Mom sees this room."

I went to get dressed. Dad usually made French toast on the weekends, and the aroma from his cooking wafted upstairs, stirring my appetite.

At breakfast, Mom reminded Amanda about going to the library for the books about vegetarianism.

"I'll come along," I said. "I have some research to do." Max, his mouth jammed with French toast, mumbled, "Me, too."

Amanda took some bananas after breakfast and went to her room to feed Angel. I followed her. The two of us watched Angel eat hungrily.

"Amanda, keep Mom with you at the library," I said. "Max and I can look through the books on primates and find out what type of monkey Angel is."

"How are you going to identify her?" Amanda asked. "There might be lots of small, greenish-brown monkeys."

"I guess we'll have to take her with us," I said.

"That's a good idea," Amanda said. "I'll tuck her into my backpack."

"You might want to take a couple of diapers, and a banana or two to keep her quiet," I suggested.

Amanda stuffed a T-shirt into the bottom of her backpack. When she put Angel inside, the monkey curled into a ball on the soft T-shirt.

"I think she's sleepy again," Amanda said. "Let's hope she'll stay quiet in the library."

At the library, Mom said, "You'd better come with me, Amanda. The best books will be in the adult section."

"We're heading downstairs to the kids' section," I said. "We need to find primate books with plenty of pictures."

"Amanda, why don't you leave your backpack with Jake?" Mom suggested. "You don't need to lug it all the way upstairs."

Amanda handed the backpack to me. "Be careful," she said. I nodded.

Chapter Seven

Angel Takes Off

Max and I headed for the kids' floor. We found the nonfiction section and searched for the books on apes and monkeys. We took several books each and sat down at a table near the window. I leaned the backpack against the wall and opened the top a little to give Angel more air. She was still fast asleep.

I opened my book and began to flip through the pages, looking for information and pictures.

"Jake, is Angel a New World monkey or an Old World monkey?" Max asked.

"Why? Are they different?"

"This book says that Old World monkeys come from Africa and Asia, and New World monkeys live in Central and South America."

I looked up from my book.

"Just look for physical descriptions, Max. Don't bother about where they come from."

"Okay," he replied. "Can you check—are Angel's nostrils small and close together?"

I lifted the flap on the backpack. Angel was curled up in a tiny ball. I could see only part of her. "I can't really tell."

"What about her tail, then?" Max asked. "Can she grab things with her tail?"

"The word is *prehensile*," I told him. "See, it tells you

here how to say it. And yes, her tail *does* grab things."

"Then she comes from the Old World, either Asia or Africa."

"That's just great!" I said. "Now we only have to check eighty-two species of Old World monkeys and find a picture of one that matches Angel."

"No, we don't," Max said. "Some of them are big guys. We just have to check the small ones like Angel."

Max is a pretty smart kid. The next few pages were filled with pictures of monkeys. We ignored the mandrills and baboons, and the black or black-and-white ones. We were careful to examine the small, brown and brownish-green monkeys.

"She could be a colobus," I said. "Let's have another look." I bent down and lifted the flap of the backpack. It was empty. Angel had disappeared!

"Oh no!" Max whispered. "How did she manage to slip away without us noticing?"

We were in real trouble. Angel could do a lot of damage in a library filled with thousands of books arranged in neat rows. Not to mention the videos and tapes and computers.

I jumped up and searched the bookshelves beside us. She wasn't in them, but half a dozen books had been pulled out and thrown onto the floor on the other side.

"Quick, Max. We have to find her," I said. "You take that side, and I'll check this one. If you see her, grab her and try to hold tight."

Max nodded and went off.

Nobody was screaming or running around. *Thank goodness!* I thought. *At least Angel must be behaving herself.*

I walked past the computers and looked in the windows of the little playhouse in the center of the large room. There were lots of stuffed toys, but no living monkey.

Then a little boy yelled, "Wow! Curious George! Look, Mommy!"

Chapter Eight

Mystery Solved!

A group of children came running in excitement. Angel was sitting on top of the guinea pig's cage, trying to get her hand through the bars. She was after the guinea pig's carrot.

Everyone started laughing and talking about Angel's diaper. It looked like it needed changing. The boy who saw Angel first was still yelling, "It's Curious George. But where's the man with the yellow hat?"

Angel jumped up and down on the cage when she couldn't reach the carrot. She chattered loudly. The guinea pig shivered in fear.

"What do we do now?" Max whispered.

"She won't come to us," I said. "Go and find Amanda, *fast!*" Max sped off.

A librarian came to see what the fuss was about. She shrieked when she saw the monkey.

"Who owns this creature?" she asked. "What's it doing here?"

"I thought it belonged to the library," replied one of the mothers.

"Oh no. We only have Jerry, the guinea pig," the librarian said. "This monkey must have escaped from the zoo or a pet store."

"Careful, Billy," one mother said to her little boy. "Monkeys have very sharp teeth."

All the parents started pulling their children back. Angel wasn't paying much attention, since she had managed to grab a small piece of the guinea pig's carrot.

The librarian was really upset.

"Close the doors so the monkey won't escape," she ordered. "I'll phone the Humane Society to come and take it away." She went behind the counter and picked up the phone.

I ran to the door and closed it. After a frantic conversation, the librarian got off the phone and told everyone to stand back away from the cage. We all stood there, watching Angel eat her carrot. She ignored the crowd around her.

I was relieved when the door opened and Mom and Amanda rushed in, with Max panting behind them. Amanda saw Angel right away and gave me a dirty look.

"Careful!" the librarian shouted. "We don't know if this animal is dangerous."

"Don't worry, it isn't," Amanda said. She walked up to Angel, stretched out her hand, and said softly, "Here, Angel, come on."

Angel hopped onto her shoulder, chattering happily. The kids laughed and clapped.

"Max, get the backpack," hissed Amanda.

"I don't think that's a good idea," the librarian said, backing away as Amanda came closer to the desk. "What if it bites you?"

She turned to Mom. "The library can't be held responsible for an injury caused by an animal that doesn't belong to us."

Mom said she thought Amanda would be safe. "The little thing looks quite peaceful," she said. "You know, I think it's a talapoin monkey."

A talapoin? I pricked up my ears, and so did Amanda and Max.

"How did you know it's a tala…whatever, Mom?" I asked.

"Talapoin," Mom replied. Then she spelled it out for us. "*T-a-l-a-p-o-i-n*. It's quite a coincidence, really," she said. "I came across the word in a crossword puzzle yesterday."

"And you looked it up in Uncle Cyrus's dictionary?" I asked.

"Yes. There was a drawing of it, too, and it certainly looked like this one."

Max, Amanda, and I looked at each other. The mystery was solved! Mom had called up Angel from the amazing dictionary without even knowing it!

I was still holding the monkey book in one hand. I

flipped over to the index and found a picture of the talapoin. It looked exactly like Angel. I skimmed through the text: "Lives in West Africa. Brownish-green. Small. White fur around the face."

We definitely had a talapoin! Now all we had to do was get the monkey and the amazing dictionary together.

Chapter Nine

Captured!

The librarian opened the door to let in the man from the Humane Society. He was carrying a very large net. Angel started to chatter when she saw him. She bounced onto Amanda's head and grabbed her hair.

"Ouch!" Amanda shouted.

"I told you it was dangerous," the librarian said. "Everyone! Stand back and let this man catch the creature."

Angel watched the man come closer. She leaped off Amanda and back to the cage.

"Now look what you've done," said Amanda. "You've scared her. Quick, Max, get a carrot from my backpack."

Amanda took the carrot and held it out toward Angel. The monkey snatched it and bounced over to the fire extinguisher.

Oh no, I thought. *I hope she doesn't take it off the hooks on the wall.* Luckily, she didn't. Instead she jumped from the fire extinguisher onto a picture, which fell to the floor with a crash. Then she took a flying leap onto the roof of the little playhouse.

"Stay calm!" the person from the Humane Society shouted. He rushed forward with his net held out, and tripped. His head and body became tangled in the net. The kids jumped up and down and laughed with delight. Mom was shaking her head. The librarian looked like she was about to explode.

Amanda walked slowly toward the monkey. She had a banana in her hand. You could see Angel wondering if she could get the fruit without being caught.

I circled around behind the playhouse with Max.

"Give me your jacket," I whispered.

Max took off his jacket and handed it to me. I crept up behind Angel with the jacket between my two hands. Just as she reached out for the banana, I dropped the jacket over her and grabbed her. I handed Angel to Amanda, who dropped her into the backpack that Max was holding open.

"Good work," said Mom. "It's almost as if you knew this monkey."

"Just using my head," I said, "like Dad always tells me to do."

Meanwhile, the man from the Humane Society had gotten himself out of the net. "I'll take the animal now," he said. "It doesn't belong to your daughter, does it?" he asked Mom.

"Of course not," Mom replied.

"Hand over the monkey," the man said. "We'll lock it up until we find out where it came from. If you follow me down to the van, I'll return your backpack when I have the monkey safely in a cage."

Amanda didn't have a choice. She handed him the backpack, and we went outside to where the Humane Society van was parked. In the back was a row of cages. The man tipped Angel into one of the cages. She looked very small and scared as the door slammed shut.

"Can we find out what happens to her?" Amanda asked.

"Just call us," the man told her. "Someone is certain to claim a valuable animal like this."

The van drove off. Now we had an even bigger problem to solve.

We were very quiet on the way home. As we got out of the car, Amanda asked Mom if we could visit the talapoin monkey at the Humane Society the next day.

"I'll take you if it's open on Saturday," Mom said. "But don't go getting any ideas about adopting it."

Amanda called the Humane Society and was told it would be open Saturday afternoon. We went to the backyard to have a conference behind the toolshed.

"Maybe we can help Angel escape," Amanda suggested.

"You can't let her run wild," I said. "She won't know how to survive here. And our winter weather will be much too cold. She comes from Africa."

"What do you suggest, then?" Amanda asked.

"I'm still thinking about it," Max said slowly. "We have to …"

"Solve the problem!" Amanda and I said together.

"Exactly!" Max frowned. He didn't think we were funny.

"Yeah, we know," I said. "But how?"

Max was silent for a while. Then he said, "We can do two things."

"What two things?" Amanda asked.

"One, we can take the amazing dictionary with us to the Humane Society and tap-tap Angel back to her home in Africa. Or two, we can smuggle Angel out of the Humane Society and bring her to the dictionary."

"We don't know if the dictionary will work outside my room," I said.

"Besides, it's too big and heavy to lug all the way to the Humane Society," Amanda added. "I suggest we smuggle Angel out somehow and bring her home. I'll take my backpack along."

We all agreed that was the best plan.

Chapter Ten

Rescue Mission

The Humane Society building was on Fairfield Street, down a long driveway. Mom dropped us there at two o'clock.

"I'll be back in an hour," she said. "Be ready outside when I come back. Uncle Luke and Aunt Beth are coming for dinner, and I have a lot to do before they arrive."

As we eagerly hopped out of the car, Mom reminded us again, "Don't get any ideas about adopting animals. Your father is allergic to cats and dogs."

But he's not allergic to monkeys, I thought. *He didn't start to sneeze and wheeze with Angel in the house.*

We asked the woman at the desk where the monkey was, and she told us to go down the hall to the cage at the very end. The hall was lined with cages packed with

dogs, and other cages with cats. The dogs stood up on their hind legs and barked or whined at us as we passed them. Some of the cats came to the front of their cages, mewing sadly. I stopped to pet them, but Max tugged at my shirt.

"Come on, we don't have all day," he said.

Amanda found Angel first.

"Over here!" she shouted. We rushed over. Angel was

in a large cage at the very back of the building. She looked miserable. The cage was closed tight with a big, shiny padlock.

"Poor Angel," Amanda said gently. "Come here and let me pet you." But Angel wouldn't come closer. Amanda showed her a plum, but still the monkey didn't move.

"I'm going to ask if I can hold her," Amanda said. "She's really upset about being caged."

Amanda went back down the hall to the front desk. We tried to coax Angel with a banana and a carrot. She looked at us and turned away.

I don't know how Amanda did it, but the woman came back with a key and unlocked the cage to let Angel out. Angel jumped out and snuggled into Amanda's hair immediately. Then she reached out for the carrot I was holding.

"Isn't that sweet," the woman cooed. "Now, be very careful not to let her go. We don't want her escaping again. I'll come back in a while to close the cage."

Amanda held Angel in her arms and stroked her. She talked softly to her.

"No time to waste," Max said. "We'll have to get Angel out of here fast."

"But the receptionist is coming back to lock her up," I said. "If she sees an empty cage, she'll know that we took Angel."

Max suggested putting a brownish cat in Angel's cage, but we didn't think a cat looked much like a monkey.

"What should we do?" Amanda asked. She had tears in

her eyes. "I just can't put her back in that cage. She'll die of loneliness."

Angel must have read that dictionary definition of monkey business. Before we knew what was happening, she jumped off Amanda's shoulder and landed on the front ledge of a cage with three cats in it. In a heartbeat, she unlatched the cage door, and the three cats leaped out with grateful meows.

Angel was delighted with herself. She skipped along the hall, opening cages on the right and the left. In a few minutes, we were surrounded by a troop of barking dogs and yowling cats. The dogs were chasing the cats, and the cats were digging their claws into the dogs.

It was like being in a crazy cartoon. I was laughing so hard that I had to lean against the side of a cage. Max was holding his stomach, and tears were rolling down his cheeks.

"Stop being idiots!" Amanda ordered. "Now is our chance to escape. Quick, grab Angel and put her in my backpack!"

I stuffed Angel into the backpack just as two Humane Society attendants came running toward us.

"What in the world happened?" one of them yelled at me.

"The monkey!" I shouted back. "It opened the cage doors."

"Where did it go?"

"That way," I pointed. "Real fast."

"Okay!" he said, and he rushed down the hallway. The other attendant was trying to herd the cats and dogs back into their cages. There was a lot of meowing and snarling. Now that they were free, the animals didn't want to be shut up in cages again.

"Walk toward the exit," whispered Amanda. "Act casual so that nobody suspects us."

We strolled past the front desk, which was empty, and

walked out the door. Then we walked quickly down the driveway to wait for Mom. We were so relieved when she pulled up.

"How was the monkey?" Mom asked as we climbed into the car.

"Up to its usual tricks," I replied.

As soon as we arrived home, Amanda, Max, and I went up to my room. We had to send the monkey back before our relatives arrived.

Amanda held Angel for the last time, patting her and scratching behind her little ears. Max stroked Angel as a way of saying good-bye.

I opened the amazing dictionary and found the drawing of the talapoin. I tapped it twice, firmly. Angel disappeared into thin air. Amanda had tears in her eyes. "She was cute, even though she *did* wreck things," she said.

"She'll be happy to be back in West Africa with the other monkeys," Max said. "Maybe you can go visit her one day."

"Come on, Amanda. We'll help you clean up your room," I said.

Later that night, I lay in bed and thought about our latest animal adventure. I was glad that Mom hadn't found out what happened when she used my amazing dictionary. I was sure that if she knew about its magical powers, she and Dad would take it away from me. Luckily, once again, everything had ended well.

Talapoin Monkey Fact Sheet

- Talapoins are small, Old World monkeys.
- They weigh a little over two pounds and are thirteen to eighteen inches tall.
- They have a long tail.
- They live in the rainforests of West Africa.
- They have excellent eyesight, hearing, and sense of smell.
- They like to live near water, and they are very good swimmers.
- They stay together in large family groups called troops.
- They enjoy eating fruit, especially berries.

For more information on talapoins, check out some of the amazing monkey websites on the Internet. Try going to a search engine and typing in the word *monkey* to see what you can find!

Using a Dictionary

You become a better reader and writer when you learn new words. Words become yours when you understand what they mean and use them in your writing and discussions.

Use a dictionary to look up any words in this book that you don't understand. You might want to start your own personal list of new words in a journal, or in a file in your computer. First, write down the definition of the word. Then use the word in a short sentence. The next time you write a short story, or an essay, try to use new words that you have learned. You will be amazed at how quickly you can expand your vocabulary this way.